A Child's Day

CRABTREE
PUBLISHING COMPANY
WWW.CRABTREEBOOKS.COM

BOBBIE KALMAN & TAMMY EVERTS

CRABTREE

PUBLISHING COMPANY

WWW.CRABTREEBOOKS.COM

Created by Bobbie Kalman

For our son Marc Crabtree, our talented photographer,
who traveled to historic villages with us and took many of the pictures
in several of our historic books, including this one.

Editor-in-Chief:
Bobbie Kalman
Writing team:
Bobbie Kalman
Tammy Everts
Editors:
David Schimpky
Lynda Hale
Petrina Gentile
Tammy Everts
Bonnie Dobkin
Janine Deschenes
Proofreader:
Crystal Sikkens
Graphic design:
Katherine Berti
Photo research:
Bobbie Kalman
Katherine Berti

Special thanks to:
The staff of Genesee Country
Museum, and Leigh Adamson and
Brian Adamson, the models who
appear throughout the book.

Photo Credits
Alamy: North Wind Picture
Archives, p5tl; Elizabeth
Whiting & Associates, p16bl
The Athenaeum: Thomas
Worthington Whittredge—
children, contents b; Theodore
Robinson—apprentice
blacksmith, p5tr; Edward Henry
Potthast—Sewing Girl, p5bl
Flickr: Sarah R, p31br
Jim Bryant: p11b
Ken Faris: p7b

Marc Crabtree: p4, p6tr, p7t,
p8b, p11tl, p16tr, p17, p22tr
**The Metropolitan Museum of
Art:** p23t from left, Brooklyn
Museum Costume Collection
at The Metropolitan Museum
of Art, Gift of the Brooklyn
Museum, 2009; Gift of Mrs.
Jason Westerfield, 1967,
Gift of Miss Mildred Natwick,
1941; Gift of Frances H. Jones,
1952; Gift of Mrs. Quincy A.
Shaw, 1988
Morgan Weistling: Feeding the
Geese, cover; Olivia's Chicken
Coop, p6b; The Prairie Church,
p20; The Snake Oil Salesman,
p29
Shutterstock: Bob Pool, p28b

Wikimedia Commons: Library of
Congress, Palmer, F. (Fanny),
1812–1876, artist; N. Currier
(Firm), publisher, American farm
scenes, p9t; Edward Lamson
Henry
—Yale University Art Gallery,
A Country School—1948.98—
Yale University Art Gallery,
p12b; Thomas Waterman Wood,
Art Institute of Chicago, p24

All other images from Shutterstock

Illustrations and colorizations
Antoinette "Cookie" Bortolon:
p9br, p10t, p13b, p14t, p15,
p18, p21br, p22b, p23b, p27
Barb Bedell: p26, p30
Crabtree Publishing: p25
Lisa Smith: p19

Library and Archives Canada Cataloguing in Publication

Title: A child's day / Bobbie Kalman & Tammy Everts.
Names: Kalman, Bobbie, author. | Everts, Tammy, 1970- author.
Series: Kalman, Bobbie. Historic communities.
Description: [Newly revised edition]. |
  Series statement: Historic communities |
  Includes index. | Previously published: 1993.
Identifiers: Canadiana (print) 2019023363X |
  Canadiana (ebook) 20190233648 |
  ISBN 9780778773108 (hardcover) |
  ISBN 9780778773207 (softcover) |
  ISBN 9781427124814 (HTML)
Subjects: LCSH: Children—North America—History—19th century—
  Juvenile literature. | LCSH: Pioneer children—North America—Juvenile literature. |
  LCSH: Frontier and pioneer life—North America—Juvenile literature.
Classification: LCC HQ781.5 .K34 2020 | DDC j305.2309709/034—dc23

Library of Congress Cataloging-in-Publication Data

Names: Kalman, Bobbie, author. | Everts, Tammy, 1970- author.
Title: A child's day / Bobbie Kalman & Tammy Everts.
Description: New York : Crabtree Publishing Company, [2020] |
  Series: Historic communities | Originally published in 1994.
Identifiers: LCCN 2019053181 (print) | LCCN 2019053182 (ebook) |
  ISBN 9780778773108 (hardcover) |
  ISBN 9780778773207 (paperback) |
  ISBN 9781427124814 (ebook)
Subjects: LCSH: Children--United States--History--19th century--Juvenile literature.
  | Pioneer children--United States--Juvenile literature. | Frontier and pioneer life--
  United States--Juvenile literature.
Classification: LCC HQ792.U5 K317 2020 (print) | LCC HQ792.U5 (ebook) |
  DDC 305.230973/09034--dc23
LC record available at https://lccn.loc.gov/2019053181
LC ebook record available at https://lccn.loc.gov/2019053182

Crabtree Publishing Company

www.crabtreebooks.com   1-800-387-7650

Printed in the U.S.A./042020/CG20200224

Published in Canada
Crabtree Publishing
616 Welland Ave.
St. Catharines, Ontario
L2M 5V6

Published in the United States
Crabtree Publishing
PMB 59051
350 Fifth Avenue, 59th Floor
New York, New York 10118

Published in the United Kingdom
Crabtree Publishing
Maritime House
Basin Road North, Hove
BN41 1WR

Published in Australia
Crabtree Publishing
Unit 3–5 Currumbin Court
Capalaba
QLD 4157

Contents

A full, busy life

Early settler children had lives that were very different from those of boys and girls today. Difficult work was a part of every day. In order to have enough food and clothing, the entire family had to work hard. Boys and girls began to do chores as soon as they were able to walk and talk. Parents loved their children, but they were very strict. They had to be—a family needed cooperation and teamwork to get everything done.

Finding time for fun

Even though boys and girls worked hard, they still found time for fun. Many children today have a huge variety of toys, games, and activities to choose from. Settler children had to amuse themselves with simple games and a few homemade toys. Most of these games were played outdoors, using objects found around the farm or in the community. An old barrel hoop provided hours of fun when it was rolled with a stick. With a bit of pretending, a fence could be a bucking horse to ride. A sturdy board laid over a tree stump became a simple seesaw. Rocks, leaves, and branches created imaginary houses and forts. A child's only limit was his or her imagination.

Are you John or Emily?

A child's life in the 1800s was both difficult and fun, but it was never dull. Pretend you are fourteen-year-old Emily (top right), or nine-year-old John (below right), who live with their parents on a small farm. Find out how their busy childhood is preparing them for their challenging lives that lie ahead.

*"Idle hands are the devil's playground" was a common saying among the early **settlers**. Children helped adults with chores, such as churning butter.*

Both boys and girls enjoyed playing with hoops.

Most girls learned skills, such as cooking, that they would need later as wives and mothers.

Clothes were made by hand, so girls learned to sew at a very young age.

Some boys became **apprentices**. They left their parents' houses to live with craftspeople, who taught them trades such as making barrels or fine silver objects. This young boy is an apprentice to a **blacksmith.**

Women and girls also washed clothes by hand. There were no washing machines in the 1800s. The clothes were first soaked in hot water and then scrubbed on a washboard. They were then rinsed and hung up to dry. In summer they were hung outdoors, and in winter, they were dried near a fireplace.

A child's day

"Goodness, John, wake up. It's five o'clock already!" Mother called upstairs. John opened his eyes, stretched quickly, and jumped out of bed—the morning chores had to be done. After dressing in his cotton shirt and comfortable trousers, John rushed out to the barn to join his father. Together, they milked the cows, cleaned the calf pens, and fed the **livestock**. After giving his favorite calf a quick pat, John returned to the house for breakfast. Emily has always loved chickens. When she was a young child, she would go to the barn just to hug them and feel their soft feathers. Emily still loves her chickens. She strokes their feathers each morning as she feeds them and collects their eggs.

John gives Daisy a treat before he goes to school.

Time for school

After breakfast, John and Emily took the lunch boxes their mother had prepared for them and walked the half-hour trek to school. There was a spelling bee that day, and Emily's team won, as usual. No one could spell as well as Emily. John was happy when the day was over because he hated to see Emily gloat!

More chores!

After school, John again enjoyed helping Father care for the animals. They spread fresh straw in the stalls of the cows, oxen, calves, pigs, and sheep so the animals could have soft, clean beds. Then, they fed the animals and milked the cows.

Chores for girls and boys

Women and girls in the nineteenth century sewed quilts, which would keep their family members warm as they slept. Girls helped their mothers spin thread, weave cloth, make candles, and sew clothing. Many families felt it was important for girls to learn how to sew when they were young.

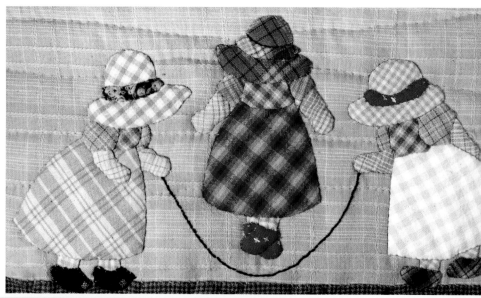

If you were Emily, what kind of design would you sew on your quilt?

Future farmers

Many boys worked outside with their fathers. They, too, would end up being farmers when they grew up. Together, the boys and their fathers plowed fields, planted crops, tamed new horses, and hunted wild birds. The boys were in charge of bringing the cows in from the pasture at night. This was a very important duty because wild animals such as wolves could kill the valuable cows.

John forgets his duty

One Saturday, John and Emily went out to pick wild strawberries. They had a contest to see who could pick the most. They were so carried away by their competition that they lost track of the time. Before bedtime that night, John remembered he had forgotten to herd the cattle back to the barn! He raced from the house to the faraway fields, listening to the wolves howling in the distance. He worried that he would be too late! Luckily, the cows were safe.

9

Time for dinner

Families looked forward to dinnertime! After a prayer of thanks was said, dinner was served. In most settler homes, the adults were served first. Finally, a heaping plate of food was put in front of each child. The plates were piled high with smoked ham, potato cakes, baked beans, **butternut squash**, **johnny cake**, and pickled beets. A favorite dish of many children was fried apples 'n' onions! Try making potato cakes and fried apples and onions by following the recipes on these pages. You'll love them both!

Potato cakes

Potato cakes are easy and fun to make. The early settlers liked them because they tasted good and used up leftover potatoes. Divide day-old cold mashed potatoes into the number of servings you wish to make. Shape the potatoes into patties. Make sure the cakes are not too thick, or they will not cook in the middle. Heat oil or bacon fat in a frying pan. Place the potato cakes in the hot fat, turning them over when the first side is brown and slightly crispy. When both sides are cooked, serve your tasty, crusty potato cakes.

John picked some apples from one of the many apple trees that grew on their farm. The apples would be used to make "fried apples'n'onions." Believe it or not, apples and onions have a delicious flavor when cooked together.

Fried apples 'n' onions

Ingredients:

8–10 slices of bacon
6 onions
6 tart apples
2 tablespoons (30mL) brown sugar

Ask an adult to help you fry the bacon slices in a **skillet**. While the bacon is cooking, peel and slice the onions. Remove the cores from the apples. Slice the apples into thin rings. Leave the skins on! They help the apples keep their shape. When the bacon is completely cooked, remove it from the skillet and set it aside on a plate. Drain most of the bacon fat from the skillet. Add the onion slices and cook them over medium-high heat for about three minutes. Spread the apple slices over the onions. Sprinkle brown sugar on top, cover the skillet, and cook for a few more minutes until the apples are tender. Stir only if it looks as if the onions are going to burn. Add the apples and onions to the bacon.

11

Going to school

As early settler communities grew, people started thinking about their children's education. Parents wanted their children to be able to read the Bible so they would become better **Christians**. Learning to **cipher**, or do arithmetic, was necessary for children who were going to be farmers, millers, craftspeople, or storekeepers. The families in growing communities built one-room schools for their children.

"Making their manners"

When students arrived at their school, their teacher was standing at the door. She smiled as the students "made their manners," which meant bowing or **curtsying** to the teacher. The youngest boys in the class sat at the front of the row of desks meant for boys. The older girls, such as Emily, sat in the middle or back of the row for girls.

Think about it

What made a teacher's job more difficult in a one-room schoolhouse? Why would having students of all ages and skill levels be a challenge?

An inky tale

One winter morning, one of the students wanted to practice writing the letters of the alphabet in his **copybook**, but he had to wait. The ink, which he had left in his desk overnight, had frozen after the stove fire was put out. Almost all the students had the same problem, so there was a row of thawing ink bottles along the top of the stove.

BANG! BANG! BANG! Huge booms filled the classroom. Many of the children screamed in terror. The ceiling was splattered with large black spots. The teacher was not happy! As she glanced at some laughing boys, she realized they had put the corks inside the ink bottles, causing them to explode. One by one, the mischief-makers were called outside by the teacher. When they came in, they were no longer laughing. The teacher had whipped them for leaving the corks in their thawing ink bottles on purpose to make them explode. The pranksters did not play tricks for quite a while after that!

Stories with a message

Emily and John loved to read. The books they read at home and school were very different from storybooks children read today. Their books contained stories with messages, or morals, about how people should behave. Called **morality tales**, these stories were supposed to teach children kindness, good manners, honesty, and respect for others. In these stories, good things happened to "good" children. Children who were considered "bad" were often taught painful lessons.

To-day's motto: "I will be thoughtful." – Winslow

What message did the teacher want these children to learn? Is this a message that children today should practice? Write five ways that you can practice being thoughtful.

A dog with manners

The following story is taken from a nineteenth-century magazine. It tells the story of a boy whose dog had better manners than he did. "Let those children, who are unwilling to help others, blush and be ashamed at the example of this noble dog."

Think about it

What moral does this story teach? Read the story and then rewrite it to show how you would have been more thoughtful.

The boy and his dog

A favorite dog, named Mungo, stood by his mistress one morning as she prepared her children, Eliza and Edmund, for school.

Eliza had been busy assisting Edmund, who now stood waiting while his mother prepared his sister as quickly as possible. As it was getting late, she asked Edmund to fetch the lunch basket. This bad-mannered boy, however, only gave a sour look. Though he did not refuse, he did not hurry to obey his mother's order.

"Well, my son," she said, "If you are unwilling to do anything for others, how can you expect others to help you? Our Mungo would bring me the basket in a moment, if he knew how."

As the mother said this, which she meant only as a scolding for her son, she was surprised to see the dog go to the closet, take the basket down from behind the door, and bring it to her side.

Simple toys, simple joys

Most children did not have many toys, so their parents encouraged them to take very good care of the ones they had. Adults believed certain toys were meant just for boys, and others just for girls. Toy soldiers, hoops, and kites were considered playthings for boys. Dolls and dollhouses were toys for girls. Both boys and girls played with toys such as puppets, marbles, checkers, and dominoes.

Not many girls were lucky enough to have a large dollhouse or such a fancy doll.

John's new stilts!

John and Emily enjoyed playing outdoors. One day, John made himself a new pair of stilts. He had outgrown his old pair. As John pictured himself walking tall on his new stilts, Emily grabbed his old pair! Even though they were a bit small, she was soon racing across the grass. She made walking on stilts seem easy. When John tried to take a few steps on his new stilts, he was surprised to discover that walking with the added height was harder than he thought it would be! Emily laughed, "You're so slow. I can walk circles around you." This made John angry and, before he knew what he was saying, he challenged his sister to a race.

The race begins

"On your mark...get set...GO!" Emily yelled, and off she raced. She was halfway across the field when she looked behind her to see how close John was. Emily gasped when she saw that John was lying on the ground with his stilts beside him! She jumped off her stilts and ran to help her brother. Emily worried that he might be badly injured.

John's clever trick

When she leaned over him to see if he was hurt, John leapt to his feet, jumped on his stilts, and started to zoom across the field. Emily was startled but began to giggle when she realized that John had tricked her. She laughed so hard that she could not finish the race. The children enjoyed the joke almost as much as they enjoyed their stilts.

The birthday party

Mother pressed John and Emily's best clothes and told them to wash their faces. The children were going to Sarah Walker's birthday party! They had never been to a party before. When they arrived at Sarah's house, several children were already there. Many of them had never been inside such a fancy house. Everyone sat nervously in Sarah's beautiful **parlor**. John and Emily were relieved when Sarah entered the room and greeted her guests. She suggested they play Blind Man's Buff. Her guests agreed enthusiastically.

Blind Man's Buff

John was It, so he put on the blindfold. The other boys and girls joined hands and skipped in a circle around him. When John called "Stop!" everyone stopped and stood still. John pointed at a person in the circle—it was Emily! She entered the circle and tried to avoid John. Though he was blindfolded, John was very tricky. He quickly tagged Emily, but he still had to guess who she was. As John touched his sister's head, he recognized the feel of the bow she was wearing in her hair. "Emily!" he shouted. Now Emily was It! The children loved this game, and they played until everyone had a chance to be It.

Cake and oranges—Yumm!

The afternoon flew by, and soon it was time for cake. The guests filed into Sarah's dining room and sat politely at the long table. No one said a word, but they were all very excited—beside each of their plates was an orange! The children weren't sure if they were allowed to eat it or if it was only meant as a decoration. When Mrs. Walker told them to enjoy their cake and orange, they couldn't believe their ears.

The cake was delicious, but a sweet, juicy orange was a rare treat! Most children received this **tropical** fruit only at Christmas! All too soon, it was time to go home. John and Emily remembered to thank Sarah and her mother for the lovely party. Then they raced home to tell Mother about the fun game, birthday cake, and delicious oranges.

19

Sunday—a special day

Most families went to church on Sunday morning. Sometimes the minister's sermon could be very long—up to three hours! After church, children were not allowed to work or play for the rest of the day. Attending church was important for most settler families. At home, parents often read Bible stories to their children, such as the one about Noah's Ark.

Noah's Ark—the story

God told Noah to build a big boat, called an ark and to put one male and one female of every kind of animal and bird into the ark. After the animals and Noah's family were in the ark, it rained without stopping for forty days and nights! The water got so deep that even the mountains were covered. Every living creature on earth died in the flood, but the ark floated on top of the flood waters. The people and animals in the ark survived and were safe.

Emily's secret Sunday work

Emily wanted to finish the **sampler** she had been working on for months. She knew she was not allowed to work on Sunday, but she couldn't understand why. She thought work was supposed to be good for her. Despite the rules, Emily decided she would do as she pleased this Sunday. She sat in the kitchen pretending to read the big family Bible, which was propped up in front of her. Hidden by the Bible, her hands were busy stitching the sampler!

Just before dinner, Emily's sampler was completed. It was beautiful, with tiny, neat, colorful stitches. She couldn't wait to show it to Mother. Emily didn't think Mother could be angry with her after seeing her lovely **embroidery**. She rose from her seat. Oh, no! By sewing so close to her lap to avoid being caught, Emily had sewn her sampler to her skirt!

When John began to laugh, Mother and Father came into the room to see what was going on. Seeing Emily's **predicament**, they also started to chuckle. The entire family had a good laugh, but Emily was still punished for working on Sunday.

One of the few toys children could play with on Sunday was a toy model of Noah's Ark. The picture above shows Noah's story. Below is a model of it. Name some of the animals that were put into the ark, using the art above as well as the toy below.

Parents thought that playing with this toy was a good Sunday pastime because the tale of Noah and his ark was a Bible story.

What did they wear?

Most boys and girls had only two outfits. During the week, boys wore comfortable cotton trousers with suspenders and a cotton shirt. Girls wore simple long dresses, which were often covered with an apron to protect the dresses from dirt and spills. Outdoors, **bonnets** protected their faces and heads from the hot sun. Girls were particularly careful about keeping their skin as light as possible. When they grew up to be women, they wanted their **complexion** to look like **porcelain**. Boys also wore hats to keep their heads from getting burned by the sun.

Girls that lived on a farm often wore simple dresses. Both boys and girls wore hats to protect them from the burning sun.

Boys wore suits such as this one made from wool. They often wore a vest under their jacket.

Young girls wore short dresses with ruffled trousers underneath, called pantelets. Most also wore aprons called pinafores, which covered most of their dresses.

In winter, many children wore coats made from blankets.

calico

Emily's new dress

Emily loved to dress in fine clothing on Sundays and special holidays. Her best dress was made of **calico**. Calico was cotton cloth printed with a bright design. For two years Emily had worn this dress, and she was getting tired of it. She wanted to ask for a new velvet dress, but she knew her parents did not have money for such a luxury. When Emily's older cousin gave her a red velvet dress that no longer fit her, Emily could not believe her good fortune. Mother offered to help alter the dress to make it Emily's size, but Emily wanted to do it by herself.

A fashion mistake!

Finally, the dress was finished. Father, Mother, and John waited for Emily to come into the kitchen wearing her grand "new" dress. Emily entered the room, but she did not look happy. Somehow, she had made errors in taking the measurements. The sleeves were different lengths, the waist was too tight, and the hem of the skirt was uneven. The dress was a disaster! John couldn't help laughing when he saw it.

Mother to the rescue!

Mother didn't make fun of Emily's mistakes. Instead, she complimented her on her tiny, neat stitching. She then offered once again to help Emily fix the dress. Together, mother and daughter sewed the hem, sleeves, and waist. When Emily tried her dress on again, it fit perfectly. She was glad she had accepted Mother's help. John liked Emily's new dress, but he found it hard not to giggle every time she wore it.

Think about it

Most children had only two outfits. Count how many outfits you have in your closet. Which two are your favorites and why?

Mr. Cole pays a visit

A visit from someone who lived outside the community was a rare event. As most settler families did not venture far outside their communities, many of these visits were from **peddlers**. Peddlers traveled from place to place selling a variety of **wares**. They were welcomed for the goods they offered—many of which were not otherwise available—but, as strangers, they were often treated with some suspicion.

Jingle, jingle, jingle

Down the road, a bell was ringing. There was, indeed, a man driving a horse and wagon to the house. It was the peddler, Mr. Cole, who came by regularly to sell his wares. Mr. Cole traveled the countryside with his goods. He sold everything from pots and pans to toys and books. His wagon was a moving general store!

Itinerant shoemakers, tinsmiths, and scissor sharpeners who traveled the countryside were other guests in settler communities.

Goods, news, and jokes

The settler families welcomed a visit from Mr. Cole. They knew that he would offer good prices on items they needed. They also looked forward to hearing news from the other communities on Mr. Cole's route. The children could not wait to hear Mr. Cole's funny jokes and stories. Sometimes he made them laugh until they cried!

The tall-tale competition

At John and Emily's home, Mr. Cole talked about a contest he had with a man in another town. The man had bet that he could tell more stories and jokes than Mr. Cole, and Mr. Cole had won the bet. John piped up, "My father knows a lot of stories. I bet he could have won that bet."

Mr. Cole's eyes twinkled. "Let's give it a try, son. If your father tells more tall tales than I do, I have some fine treats for you and your sister." The contest began. For every story or joke Mr. Cole told, Father also had a story or joke. Finally, Mr. Cole stopped.

A good sport

"I'm out of stories," he said. "You win!" From his bag of goods, Mr. Cole pulled two small bags of candy—one for Emily, and one for John. The children were proud of their father, but they felt badly for Mr. Cole, who had lost the contest. "Cheer up," he told them, laughing. "Now I have one more story—I can tell folks about the time I was beaten at storytelling!"

Books, brushes, toys, and tools could all be found on a peddler's wagon. What might John and Emily have wanted their parents to buy from Mr. Cole?

The country fair

After the autumn harvest, everyone looked forward to the country fair. John and his family were excited as they dressed in their Sunday best. Emily had entered some of her **preserves** in a contest and hoped to win a prize. John couldn't wait to see the horse races. Father looked forward to talking about crops and cattle with other farmers. Mother was happy to visit with her friends, whom she rarely saw. The women worked together to prepare the potluck dinner.

Potlucks were shared meals in which every person or family brought something to eat.

An exciting race

The day passed quickly. The final event—the horse race—was approaching. The crowd at the racetrack admired the beautiful horses with long legs and necks, glossy coats, and quick steps.

Runaway horses!

BOOM! The gun went off, signaling the start of the race. Unfortunately, the shot scared the horses, and caused them to veer off the path and race through the crowd at full speed. Some mischievous boys had pushed over a barrel of apples, sending the fruit sprawling toward the feet of the horses. Now the frightened horses were out of control and heading straight for the tent where the women were preparing dinner!

The men in the crowd chased the horses, but the terrified animals were much too fast. Even their riders hung on for dear life! One of the women came out of the tent, wondering what all the noise was about. The crowd was very worried that she would be trampled by the racing horses. The woman had only seconds to react. As the horses approached, she flapped her apron at them. They were so startled that they changed direction again and ran toward an open field, where their riders were able to bring them under control. As the horses calmed down, the woman looked up at the crowd and asked, "What are you all looking at? Dinner's getting cold!"

A trip to town

Every autumn, Emily and John's father took grain to the **gristmill** to be ground into flour. The gristmill was located outside the town. It used the power of the fast-flowing river to operate its machinery. Mr. Harper, the gristmill owner, was a very important man in the community.

The fascinating gristmill

Sometimes Father let Emily and John come to the gristmill with him. Visiting the mill was exciting. Emily and John stared in awe at the complicated machinery. Emily liked to play with the mill cat. The cat's job was to catch the mice and rats that ate the grain. Emily also liked to stand on the miller's scale to see how much she weighed.

The blacksmith's forge

On some trips to town, Emily and John visited Mr. Reilly, the blacksmith. The blacksmith was a craftsperson who made everything from cooking **utensils** to nails and horseshoes. His workroom was filled with many different tools and gadgets, such as hammers, mallets, and **tongs** of all shapes and sizes. Many items in John and Emily's house had been made by Mr. Reilly. At the general store, Father also ordered iron items that Mr. Reilly did not have time to make.

As water runs over the mill wheel, the wheel turns and powers the huge millstones inside. The grain is ground between the stones as they spin in opposite directions.

*This blacksmith is working at a raised brick fireplace, called the forge. He holds the iron in the fire with long tongs. When the iron is soft, he hammers it into horseshoes or tools on a heavy iron block called an **anvil**.*

To market, to market

Farmers made weekly trips into town to sell their goods, such as fruits and vegetables, meat and eggs, and baskets. Sometimes Father took Emily and John with him to help out at the market. It was an exciting place, filled with things to see and do. Emily loved to look at the beautiful goods made by local craftspeople, such as clothing and quilts.

Snake oil?

Sometimes, merchants drove wagons to town selling products such as snake oil. Snake-oil salesmen told people that the oil was a cure for many kinds of illnesses. People bought the oil because they wanted to believe they would be cured. Many health products today are sold in a similar way. Do some research and find some products that are fake and write three ways that people try to sell them.

An exciting day!

Father had told Emily and John that they could visit the shops after they had unloaded the wagon. Emily and John walked happily down the street, looking in the shop windows, marveling at everything they saw. Inside the general store, the walls were lined with shelves that were filled with everything from cloth, medicine, toys, spices, and candy, as well as soap, clothes, dishes, and tools. As Emily admired some fabric, John looked greedily at the candy jars.

After a long, exciting day, John felt happy that night. When he came home, Mother had a delicious supper waiting, after which he ate the candy he bought at the store. He felt cozy in his warm bed. Perhaps he and his father would go fishing tomorrow, after the chores were finished. Emily called "good night" to him from her room. Although he would never admit it, John was happy to have Emily as his sister.

Activity

Making butter

The lives of settler children were busy. Chores took up much of their day. To get an idea of the kind of work they had to do, try your hand at making butter.

Early settlers made their own butter using cream from cow's milk. The cream was put into a butter churn, which was a tall barrel with a long pole inserted through the top. The pole, which had a plunger or paddle at the bottom, was moved up and down as quickly as possible to churn the cream. (See page 4.) Eventually, the cream thickened and became butter.

You can make your own butter using materials you have around your home.

What you'll need

- a small, clean jar with a tight, screw-on lid. A jelly jar works well.

- ½ pint (236 mL) of heavy cream (or whipping cream)

- one or two marbles to help shake up the cream

- a pinch of salt for taste

- a spoonful of honey (optional)

What you'll do

1. Put the marbles into the jar. Fill the jar with the cream and screw the top on tightly.

2. Begin shaking the jar as quickly as possible. Keep shaking for at least 15 minutes. Solid lumps will begin to form.

3. Drain the liquid from the jar. This liquid is called "buttermilk." Make sure you remove all the marbles!

4. Taste the butter. Add a bit of salt or honey, if you like.

Spread your butter on a cracker or bread and enjoy. Now, imagine having to do this every time you run out of butter!

Glossary

Note: Some boldfaced words are defined where they appear in the book.

apprentice A person who learns a skill by working for a craftsperson

blacksmith A craftsperson who makes goods from iron

bonnet A hat with strings that tie under the chin

butternut squash A large, pear-shaped, orange vegetable

Christian A person who follows the teachings of Jesus Christ

complexion The color and texture of the skin on the face

copybook A notebook in which children practiced their handwriting

curtsying Moving in a similar way to a bow to show respect

embroidery Decorative sewing done with colored thread

itinerant Describing someone who travels from place to place

johnny cake A flat cake made of cornmeal

livestock Farm animals

noble Generous and dignified

parlor A sitting room, usually used for entertaining visitors

porcelain A type of fine china, white in color

predicament A difficult situation

preserves Fruits and vegetables treated with sugar or other additives to keep them fresh for a long time

sampler A piece of embroidery done in different stitches to show sewing skill

settler A person who moves with a group of others to live in a new country or area

skillet A flat frying pan

tongs A tool with two arms used for grasping objects

tropical Relating to the hot region near the equator

utensil An instrument or container used in the kitchen

wares Articles offered for sale

Index